Table of Contents

Introduction

What is an electronic pressure cooker?

Electric pressure cookers are extremely time-saving, efficient, and flexible cooking apparatuses. These pressure cookers are a good investment because if you keep them with care and use, according to instruction, then they will stay with you for many years. Obviously, let us not overlook that they are not only things to adorn your kitchen with-they have an exceptionally extraordinary reason and a stunning cluster of advantages which you will definitely make you happy.

If you are not very fond of pressure cooker, now may be a great opportunity to make it a propensity for cooking always with these modern techniques. According to dietitians and health specialists, electric pressure cooking dependable results to more beneficial and more delicious food. The thick and tight top of them keep the steam and weight inside, the vitamins and nutrients of food stay inside the cooker. Furthermore, keeping heat in a specific area also accelerates the cooking procedure.

Advantages of using Electric pressure Cooker

There are different advantages which electric pressure cookers are known to have. In many cases, you don't have to use cooking oil in them because of the weight of the cooker, natural oils of vegetables and meats are being used for cooking. Therefore, you get the food that is more nutritious and delicious.

Health Benefits

For health point of view or people who need to get fit, this pressure cooking is a perfect option among the most preferred cooking techniques for making meals. These cookers have a tendency to contain a less fat and cholesterol contrasted with food that is fried or cooked with the common stainless-steel pot.

Compactness

When it comes to compactness, these cookers are known to be an impeccable companion for outdoors trips and other adventure because it will not only save your time but also will give you very delicious, healthy food.

Flexibility is another component that makes them perfect for any family. If you are interested in cooking and want to cook new foods and recipes, electric pressure cookers will give you the right add-on accessories.

Hence, it is one of the great innovations that are essential for any kitchen. These cookers have become a must part of the kitchen because for working moms there is nothing better than these wonderful and time saving cookers. They have high tech safety valves and also have a pushdown pressure system which helps to cook. By producing some sound it warns you if something goes wrong. They mostly operate the pressure range between seventy to eight kilopascal and you prepare the food in a short time. You can cook various foods such as meat, vegetables, broccoli, dry beans, corn and much more in these electric pressure cookers.

Breakfast Recipes

Pressure Cooker Hard Boiled Breakfast Eggs

Prep Time: 1minute
Cook Time: 5-6 minutes
Serve: 6

Ingredients:

6 extra large chilled fresh eggs

Directions:

With one cup of water, fill the electric pressure cooker pot.
Put inside the trivet, egg stand and eggs.
Close the lid of the pressure cooker.
At low pressure cook the eggs for 5 minutes.
Open the lid and have a natural release.

Put the eggs inside filled with cold water and keep the pot under running tap water.
Peel carefully by tapping the two corner sides and the middle of the eggs.

NUTRITION INFORMATION

Calories: 86
Total fat: 6 g
Carbohydrate: 0.4 g
Protein: 7 g Strawberry & Creamed Roll Oats in Pressure Cooker

Strawberry & Creamed Roll Oats in Pressure Cooker

Prep Time: 5 minutes
Cook Time: 10 minutes
Serve: 1

Ingredients:

2/3 cup whole milk
1/3 cup rolled oats
2 tablespoon dried and frozen strawberries
½ teaspoon white sugar
1 pinch salt

Directions:

Make the electric pressure cooker ready with water and steamer basket.
In a heat-proof small bowl, add milk, oats, salt and strawberries.
Close the lid of the cooker.
At high pressure, cook for 10 minutes.
At the beep, have a natural release. Unplug the cooker. Open when the indicator goes down.
Mix all the contents, sprinkle the sugar and serve.

NUTRITION INFORMATION

Calories: 95
Total fat: 4.5 g
Carbohydrate: 4.4 g
Protein: 3.3 g

Pressure Cooker Rum Chestnut

Prep Time: 45 minutes
Cook Time: 40 minutes
Serve: 5

Ingredients:

300g white sugar
750g fresh chestnuts
Rum liquor
300g water

Directions:

Peel the chestnuts after halving.
Write down the weighing of the chestnuts after weighing ti in the pressure cooker.
Now put half of chestnut's weigh water and sugar.
Close the lid and cook for 20 minutes on high pressure.
When it beeps, unplug the cooker and open when indicator gets down.

Add rum and puree the elements by tilting the cooker pot and blend till desired consistency.
Serve to use like jelly or jam.

NUTRITION INFORMATION

Calories: 110
Total fat: 2.0 g
Carbohydrate: 9.4 g
Protein: 1.5 g

Breakfast Bread in Pressure Cooker

Prep Time: 10 min
Cook Time: 20 min
Serve: 5

Ingredients:

2 Cups all purpose flour
1 Tea Spoon olive oil
½ Baking soda
1 ¼ Cup yogurt1 teaspoon salt
Water

Directions:

Prepare the electric pressure cooker with a steamer.
Take a 4 cup long container and oil it with olive oil.
In a bowl add flour, salt and baking soda. Stir all and add yogurt. Then knead. The mixture has to be flaky and chunky.
Gather the dough and make a ball. It will be sticky, if not, add water.
Make it longer and put it in the oiled container, add oil splash on the top.
Cover with foil and lower it in the cooker, fill the cooker with hot water to the mid height of the container.
Lock the lid.
Cook on high pressure for 25 minutes.
When the beep sounds, unplug the cooker and open when the pressure indicator gets down.
Remove the container and foil carefully and taste the bread with a toothpick.
Slice and serve.

NUTRITION INFORMATION

Calories: 105
Total fat: 0.3 g
Carbohydrate: 7.5 g
Protein: 0.5 g

Pressure Cooker Butter Maple Syrup Oats

Prep Time: 3 minutes
Cook Time: 20 minutes
Serve: 1

Ingredients:

¾ Cups of water
¼ Cups of oats
½ Tablespoon butter
1 Pinch salt
1 Tablespoon maple syrup

Directions:

Prepare the electric pressure cooker with steamer basket and 2 cups of water.
Add oats, salt, butter and water in a small heat-proof bowl.
Close the lid.
Cook on high pressure for 3 minutes.

Unplug the cooker and open when the indicator gets down. Mix the elements and pour on maple syrup to serve.

NUTRITION INFORMATION

Calories: 87

Total fat: 1.6 g

Carbohydrate: 9.1 g

Protein: 0.8 g

Pressure Cooker Vanilla Espresso Chocolate Oats

Prep Time: 5 minutes
Cook Time: 20 minutes
Serve: 4

Ingredients:

1 Cup milk
2 ½ Cups water
1 Cup steel cut oats
1 Tablespoon espresso powder
2 Tablespoon sugar
2 Teaspoon vanilla extract
¼ Teaspoon salt
Finely grated chocolate
Freshly whipped cream

Directions:

To the electric pressure cooking pot, add oats, milk, water, espresso powder, sugar and salt.
Stir to dissolve the powder.
Lock the lid
Cook for 10 minutes on high pressure.
When the beep makes sound, unplug it and wait for five minutes to get the pressure low.
Stir additional sugar and vanilla extract.
Let the oats get thick by letting it sit for 5 minutes.
Serve with whipped cream and chocolates on top.

NUTRITION INFORMATION
Calories: 120
Total fat: 2.8 g
Carbohydrate: 12 g
Protein: 2.5 g

Pressure Cooker Blueberry Compote

Prep Time: 5 minutes
Cook Time: 25 minutes
Serve: 2 cups

Ingredients:

3 or 4 cup sugar
3 Cups frozen blueberries
2 Tablespoon cornstarch
2 Tablespoon water
2 Tablespoon lemon juice

Directions:

To electric pressure cooking pot, add lemon juice, blueberries and sugar.
Stir to combine.

Lock the lid and cook for 3 minutes on high pressure.
When the beep makes sound, have a natural release for 10 minutes.
After 10 minutes have a quick release.
Whisk water and cornstarch in a small bowl.
Add the mixture in the cooking pot.
Set sauté function and bring to boil.
Stir constantly.
Put in a container cool in both room temperature and the refrigerator before serving.

NUTRITION INFORMATION
Calories: 95
Total fat: 0.2 g
Carbohydrate: 9 g
Protein: 0.3 g

Pressure Cooker Apple Brown Sugar Steel Cut Oats

Prep Time: 10 minutes
Cook Time: 35 minutes
Serve: 4-6

Ingredients:

1 Cup steel cut oats
1 Tablespoon butter
3 ½ Cups water
2 Tablespoons light brown sugar
1 Large peeled, cored and diced apple
¼ Teaspoon salt
1 ½ Teaspoon ground cinnamon

Directions:

Select sauté and add butter to electric pressure cooking pot. When the butter melts, add oats and toast, stir till it gets dark and nutty for 3 minutes.

Add apples, water, brown sugar, salt and cinnamon. Cook for 10 minutes on high pressure.

When the beep makes sound, have a natural release for 10 minutes and then have a quick pressure release.

Remove the lid, stir oats, again cover and let the oats sit for 10 minutes.

Serve with nuts, milk and additional brown sugar being topped.

NUTRITION INFORMATION

Calories: 108

Total fat: 1.3 g

Carbohydrate: 10.2 g

Protein: 0.8 g

Pressure Cooker Quick Breakfast Quinoa

Prep Time: 5 minutes
Cook Time: 15 minutes
Serve: 6

Ingredients:

2 ¼ Cups of water
1 ½ Cups uncooked well rinsed quinoa
½ Teaspoon vanilla
2 Tablespoons maple syrup
Pinch salt
¼ Teaspoon ground cinnamon
Fresh berries to taste
Sliced almonds to taste
Milk to serve

Directions:

To the electric pressure cooking pot, add water, quinoa, vanilla, cinnamon, maple syrup and salt.
Cook for 1 minute on high pressure.
With the sound of beep, have a quick release and wait for 10 minutes.
Open the lid to let the steam disperse.
Serve with berries, sliced almonds and milk after fluffing the quinoa.

NUTRITION INFORMATION
Calories: 108
Total fat: 2.8 g
Carbohydrate: 9.5 g
Protein: 0.8 g

Delicious Pressure Cooker Lemon Blue Berry Steel cut oats

Prep Time: 10 minutes
Cook Time: 25 minutes
Serve: 4

Ingredients:

1 Cup steel cut oats
1 Tablespoon butter
½ Cup half and half
3 Cups of water
1 Tablespoon lemon zest
2 Tablespoon sugar
¼ Teaspoon salt
¼ Cup chia seeds
1 Cup of frozen blueberries

Directions:

Select sauté after adding butter to the pot of the electric pressure cooker.
When the butter melts, add oats and toast.
Stir constantly for 3 minutes till smell nutty.
Add half and half, zest, sugar, water and salt.
Cook for 10 minutes on high pressure.
With the sound of beep, turn it off and have a natural pressure release for 10 minutes and also a quick release.
Remove the lid. Stir oats, chia seeds and blueberries. Cover again and let the oats sit for dried thickness.
Serve with being topped by sliced almonds, honey, blueberries etc.

NUTRITION INFORMATION
Calories: 105
Total fat: 1.3 g
Carbohydrate: 8g
Protein: 0.35 g

Bread Recipes

Pressure Cooker Coconut Almond Cranberry Loaf

Prep Time: 15 minutes
Cook Time: 10 minutes
Serve: 4

Ingredients:

1 Cup coconut flour
1 tsp unrefined sea salt
4 Eggs
1/4 Cup coconut oil
½ Cup cranberries, raisins and almonds
1/4 Cup tapioca flour
1 tsp baking soda

Directions:

Chop the almonds, cranberries and set aside for now.
Whisk the eggs in a mixing bowl.
Add the oil, tapioca flour, coconut flour, sea salt and baking soda.
Mix well into a batter.
Add the chopped nuts and pour into your greased loaf pan.
Add to the electric pressure cooker and cook on low heat for about 10 minutes.
Let it cool down before taking out of the loaf pan. Serve cold or in room temperature.

NUTRITION INFORMATION
Calories: 140
Total fat: 2 g
Carbohydrate: 20.4 g
Protein: 1.5 g

Pressure Cooker Delicious dinner Rolls

Prep Time: 15 minutes
Cook Time: 10 minutes
Serve: 4

Ingredients:

1/2 Cups of warm water
1 Cup of arrowroot flour
1 tbsp yeast
1/2 tsp unrefined sea salt
1/2 Cup of coconut oil
½ Cup of coconut flour
2 Eggs, beaten until frothy

Directions:

In a mixing bowl combine the warm water with yeast and flour. Mix well and let it sit for 30 minutes.

Add in the eggs, coconut oil, sea salt and arrowroot flour. Knead into a soft dough.

Make small dinner rolls and add to your round baking dish.

Add the dish to your electric pressure cooker and cook on low heat for just 10 minutes.

Serve warm.

NUTRITION INFORMATION

Calories: 125

Total fat: 3.2 g

Carbohydrate: 18 g

Protein: 2.5 g

Pressure Cooker Banana Bread

Prep Time: 15 minutes
Cook Time: 8 minutes
Serve: 4

Ingredients:

1 ½ Cups blanched almond flour
½ tsp vanilla essence
2 Eggs
½ tsp sea salt
½ tsp baking soda
1 tsp coconut oil
2 Ripe bananas

Directions:

Peel the bananas and mash them finely.
Whisk the eggs in a mixing bowl.
Add in the vanilla, sea salt, baking soda and coconut oil.
Fold in the almond flour and mix gently.
Finally, add the mashed banana and knead into a soft dough.
Add it to your loaf pan.
Add the pan into an electric pressure cooker.
Cook for only 8 minutes with low heat.
Release the pressure and let it cool down.
Serve in room temperature.

NUTRITION INFORMATION
Calories: 160
Total fat: 4.3 g
Carbohydrate: 17.9 g
Protein: 3.4 g

Pressure Cooker Pumpkin Bread

Prep Time: 15 minutes
Cook Time: 20 minutes
Serve: 6

Ingredients:

1 1/2 Cups of almond flour
1 Cup of fresh pumpkin purée
1/2 Teaspoon ginger
1/4 Cup of coconut flour
1/2 Teaspoon of nutmeg
4 Eggs
1 Teaspoon of cinnamon
1/2 Cup Palm oil
1/2 Teaspoon of salt
1/3 Cup raw honey
1 Teaspoon of baking soda
1/2 Teaspoon of apple cider vinegar

Directions:

Whisk the eggs in a large bowl using an electric whisker.
Add in the ginger, nutmeg, honey, baking soda, vinegar, and pumpkin puree.
Mix well and add the rest of the ingredients.
Mix into a fine dough and make sure it is not too runny but is sticky enough.
Add to your baking dish.
Add the dish to your electric pressure cooker and cook for about 20 minutes on low heat.
Release the pressure manually and wait for it to cool down.
Cut into slices when cools down and serve.

NUTRITION INFORMATION
Calories: 273
Total fat: 11 g
Carbohydrate: 24 g
Protein: 8 g

Pressure Cooker Bread Roll with Raspberry Jam

Prep Time: 15 minutes
Cook Time: 30 minutes
Serve: 6

Ingredients:

1 Cup of almond butter
½ Cup of milk
2 Cup almond flour
3Eggs
1/4 Cup coconut flour
½ Cup raspberry jam
A pinch of salt
1/4 Cup lemon juice

Directions:

Beat the butter in a bowl.
Add in the eggs one at a time and beat until smooth.
Add the coconut flour, almond flour, salt and mix well.
Add the lemon juice and milk and knead into a fine dough.
Roll them using your hands and add one spoonful of raspberry jam in the middle.
Add the bread rolls onto your baking dish.
Add to an electric pressure cooker and cook on low heat for about 12 minutes.
Manually release the pressure and serve in room temperature.

NUTRITION INFORMATION

Calories: 167
Total fat: 5 g
Carbohydrate: 22 g
Protein: 2.3 g

Meat Recipes

Recipes Pressure Cooker Mutton Rice and Vegetable

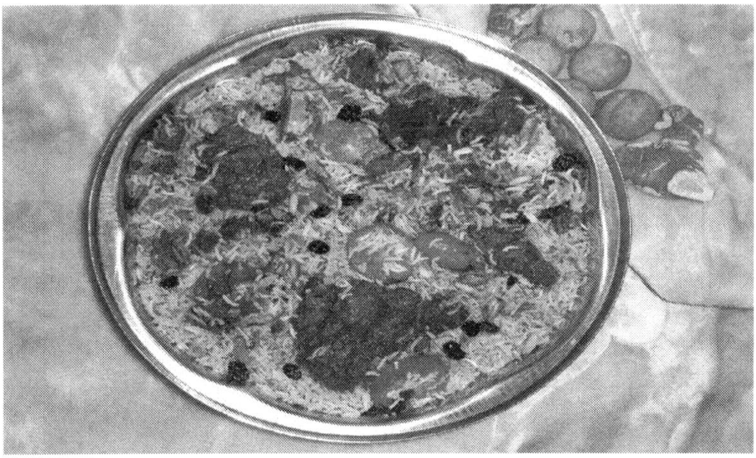

Prep Time: 20 minutes
Cook Time: 40 minutes
Serve: 6

Ingredients:

8 Mutton pieces
1 Tablespoon of curates
3 Tomatoes, diced
2 Tablespoon of turmeric
Fresh herbs
2 Tablespoon of ginger garlic paste
3 Red chilies
1½ Cups of rice
6 Green chilies
2 Tablespoon of allspice
4 Tablespoon of olive oil
Salt to taste

½ Teaspoon of cumin
2 Diced Onions
2 Tablespoons of onion paste

Directions:

In an electric pressure cooker, add half the oil.
Add the rice and cover with the cooker lid.
Set the timer to 8 minutes with high pressure.
Let the pressure release manually.
Transfer the rice into a bowl.
The same pressure cooker, add the rest of the oil.
Add the onion, onion paste, cumin, allspice, chilies, tomatoes, ginger garlic paste and turmeric.
Add ½ cup of water and stir well.
Cover with the lid again and set the timer to 5 minutes on medium heat.
Release the pressure and add the mutton pieces.
Cover again and set the timer to 12 minutes with medium heat.
Let the pressure release naturally this time.
Now add the rice, herbs and curates.
Cover again and set the timer to 5 minutes with low heat.
Wait for the pressure to get naturally and let the dish sit on the stove without any flame for 10 minutes.
Serve hot.

NUTRITION INFORMATION

Calories: 195
Total fat: 8.2 g
Carbohydrate: 13.4 g
Protein: 14.5 g

Pressure Cooker Beef Carrot Curry

Prep Time: 15 minutes
Cook Time: 30 minutes
Serve: 6

Ingredients:

1 Small onion, minced
2 Cups of water
5 Carrots, chopped
1 Tablespoon of olive oil
2 Pounds of cubed beef stew meat
2 Cubes of beef bouillon
8 Carrots
Salt to taste

Directions:

Warm up the oil in the pressure cooker on a medium-high flame.
If the cooker has an insert, remove it and cook in the bottom.

Add the onion and beef and cook till they turn golden brown.
Add in the water, bouillon cubes and carrots.
Top up the cooker with a lid and set the pressure regulator.
Cook till the Ingredients sizzle and reduce the flame to medium level.
Add the carrots, and cook to make them soft and juicy.

NUTRITION INFORMATION
Calories: 350
Total fat: 12 g
Carbohydrate: 20.4 g
Protein: 15 g

Pressure Cooker Mexican Beef Enchiladas

Prep Time: 15 minutes
Cook Time: 40 minutes
Serve: 6

Ingredients:

1 Cup of salsa
2 Tablespoons of apple cider vinegar
1 ½ Cup of beef broth
1 Teaspoon of garlic powder
1 Teaspoon of chili powder
1 Teaspoon of onion powder
1-3 Pounds of chuck beef roast
1 Teaspoon of salt
½ Teaspoon of pepper
1 ½ Cups of grated Mexican cheese blend
1 Teaspoon of ground cumin
2 Tablespoons of cornstarch
3 Tablespoons of water

10 Pieces of 6” tortillas

Directions:

Combine the beef broth, onion powder, garlic powder, chili powder, vinegar, salsa, cumin, salt and pepper into the electric pressure cooker.

Pour in the beef and cook in high pressure.

Remove the beef from the pressure cooker and chop with a fork to discard any fat.

In a small bowl, mix up the water and corn starch to form a smooth paste.

Separate any form of fat from the liquid portion.

Jumble the corn starch paste in to the cooking liquid.

Cook till the sauce becomes a bit dense.

Mix ½ cup of sauce with the minced beef.

Spread about ½ cup of sauce onto your pan.

Add shredded beef in the middle of the tortilla. Then add 1 tablespoon of cheese.

Roll up and add to the pan. Pour in the sauce.

Top the enchiladas with some extra cheese and bake for 20 minutes at 350 degrees.

Let them come to room temperature and serve.

NUTRITION INFORMATION

Calories: 245

Total fat: 11 g

Carbohydrate: 13 g

Protein: 14 g

Pressure Cooker Mongolian Beef

Prep Time: 10 minutes
Cook Time: 15 minutes
Serve: 6-8

Ingredients:

2 Pounds steak
1 Tablespoon olive oil
½ Cup of water
2 Tablespoons of cornstarch
½ Cup of soy sauce
3 Garlic cloves, minced
3 Tablespoons of water
3 Onions, diced
½ Teaspoon of fresh ginger, chopped
Salt and Pepper

Directions:

Flavor beef with salt and pepper
Add in oil in the electric pressure cooker and set for browning.
Cook all the meats in batches till they become brownish. Put them aside in a bowl.
Roll in the ginger and fry for one minute.
Jumble all the other Ingredients except cornstarch, water and onions. Mix up smoothly.
Combine the cornstarch and water in a smooth paste.
Cook the beef with its accumulated juice on a high pressure for another 15 minutes.
Pour in the cornstarch paste whisking continuously.
Parboil the whole mixture and rill in the onions before serving.

NUTRITION INFORMATION
Calories: 165
Total fat: 7.6 g
Carbohydrate: 17.2 g
Protein: 25 g

Pressure Cooker Beef Stroganoff

Prep Time: 10 minutes
Cook Time: 20 minutes
Serve: 8-10

Ingredients:

2 Pounds of beef round steak
1 Onion, minced
1 Tablespoon of almond butter
2 Cloves of garlic, diced
1 Tablespoon of olive oil
1 ½ Cups of beef broth
12 Ounces of mushrooms, diced
Egg noodles, cooked
2 Tablespoons of tomato paste
3 Tablespoons of cold water
2 Tablespoons of cornstarch

1/3 Cups of Greek Yogurt
Salt and pepper to taste

Directions:

Cut the beef into medium chunks. Flavor beef with salt and pepper.
In an electric pressure cooker pour in the oil and cook them in till they turn brown. Set them aside in a plate.
Add in the onions, garlic and tomato paste.
Add the beef broth and scrap up any brownish bits on the bottom of the electric pressure cooker.
Add the browned beef. Cook in high pressure for 10 minutes.
Meanwhile, warm up almond butter and oil in a fry pan on a medium-high flame.
Shallow fry the white mushrooms till they become golden.
Mix up the cornstarch and cold water to make a smooth paste.
Add in the paste to the beef broth and blend well. Parboil till the sauce becomes dense.
Combine the gravy into the Greek Yogurt.
Add in the mushrooms. Dish out over egg noodles.

NUTRITION INFORMATION
Calories: 185
Total fat: 9.3 g
Carbohydrate: 19.2 g
Protein: 22.1 g

Bone In Beef Short Ribs

Prep Time: 15 minutes
Cook Time: 50 minutes
Serve: 4

Ingredients:

2 Tablespoons olive oil
2 Smoked chicken, sliced
4 Large beef short ribs
1 Finely chopped onion
3 Minced garlic gloves
1 Cup of beef broth
1.5 Cup of apple juice
2 Tablespoon of tomato paste
1 Tablespoon of cornstarch
1 Tablespoon water

Directions:

With salt and pepper, season the ribs. Selecting browning, add oil to electric pressure cooker. After the oil gets hot, brown them one after one and put them in a plate.

Now put chicken in the pot and fry them till crisp and brown.

Add onions to the pot and sauté for 3 minutes till tender.

Now add the apple juice and then scrape the bottom of the pot.

Then one by one add the broth, tomato paste and the rib to the pot and lock the lid.

Select 40 minutes cooking time in high pressure.

After 40 minutes, do a natural pressure release for 10 minutes.

Remove ribs with tongs to a platter and foil them to keep warm.

To separate the fat, use a fat separator. Now put the juice again to the pot.

After that, mix cornstarch and water in a small bowl.

Now mix them with the juice in the pot.

Bring to brown after selecting sauté .Stir constantly till it thickens.

Turn the pot off. Stir to coat with sauce after adding ribs.

Let the sauce to be absorbed by the ribs after putting the lid back on for 10 minutes.

Serve with noodles or mashed potatoes.

NUTRITION INFORMATION

Calories: 325

Total fat: 5.6 g

Carbohydrate: 17.4 g

Protein: 28.1 g

Pressure Cooker Beef and Broccoli

Prep Time: 10 minutes
Cook Time: 20 minutes.
Serve: 6

Ingredients:

1 ½ lbs. beef cut into slices
1 Onion, minced
1/3 Cup of brown sugar
3 Tablespoons of cornstarch
2 Tablespoons of sesame oil
3 Tablespoons of water
1/8 Tablespoon red pepper flakes
¾ Cup of beef broth
2 Tablespoons of olive oil
1 lb broccoli florets
½ Cup of soy sauce

Salt and pepper to taste
4 Garlic cloves, minced

Directions:

Flavor the beef with salt and pepper.
Put the oil in the electric pressure cooker and fry the meat till they attain brownish hue.
Now add in the onions and garlic. Cook till they are melted.
Add sesame oil, soy sauce, brown sugar, red pepper flakes and beef broth. Whisk till the sugar gets dissolved completely.
Cook in a high pressure for 12-15 minutes.
Put the broccoli in a microwave safe bowl and add in ¼ cup of water. Microwave till the florets become soft.
Make a liquid out of the cornstarch and water. Roll it in to the pot and mix up smoothly. Cook till the gravy thickens.
Now pour in the microwaved broccolis.
Serve with hot, cooked rice. You can use sesame seeds for decoration if you want to.

NUTRITION INFORMATION
Calories: 245
Total fat: 8.4 g
Carbohydrate: 18 g
Protein: 21.3 g

Pressure Cooker Creamy Chili Chicken

Prep Time: 10 minutes
Cook Time: 20 minutes.
Serve: 6-8

Ingredients:

2 Teaspoon garlic powder
1 Teaspoon of onion powder
1 Teaspoon of chili powder
½ Cup of chicken broth
2 Cups of heavy cream
1 Teaspoon of paprika
1 Teaspoon of salt
2 Tablespoons of almond butter
2 Tablespoons of oil
2 lbs. chicken tenders
2 Tablespoons of water
2 Tablespoons of cornstarch
2 Tablespoons parsley
10 oz cooked spaghetti

Directions:

In a mixing bowl mix up salt, pepper, onion, chili and garlic powder, paprika.
Roll in the chicken and top with spices.
Warm up the oil and almond butter in the electric pressure cooker.
Shallow fry the chicken and add in the chicken broth and cook in high pressure.
In a small bowl, mix up cornstarch and water. Pour the mixture over the chicken and whisk to combine. Cook till the gravy thickens. Remove from the heat and blend in the Greek Yogurt.
Dish out with spaghetti drizzled with parsley.

NUTRITION INFORMATION
Calories: 180
Total fat: 6.5 g
Carbohydrate: 21 g
Protein: 22 g

Hot Chicken Wings in Pressure Cooker

Prep Time: 5 minutes
Cook Time: 30 minutes.
Serve: 8

Ingredients:

2 Pounds of chicken wings and drumettes
½ Cup of any BBQ sauce

Directions:

Cook the wings and drumettes on a high pressure for 5 minutes in an electric pressure cooker.
Add in the BBQ sauce and cover again with lid.
Cook for another 5 minutes.
Serve hot.

NUTRITION INFORMATION
Calories: 155

Total fat: 6 g
Carbohydrate: 1.4 g
Protein: 8 g

Pressure Cooker Orange Rice Wine Chicken

Prep Time: 5 minutes
Cook Time: 10 minutes.
Serve: 4

Ingredients:

½ Cup of orange marmalade
2 Tablespoon of brown sugar
1 Teaspoon of sesame oil
¼ Cup + 3 tablespoons of water
1 Tablespoon of rice wine vinegar
2 Onions, diced
Red pepper flakes optional
3 Tablespoons of cornstarch
¼ Cup of soy sauce
4 Large boneless chicken breasts

Directions:

Add all the Ingredients except cornstarch, 3 tablespoons of water and marmalade in the electric pressure cooker.
Cook on a high pressure for 3 minutes.
Now add the marmalade and blend well to combine.
Mix up the cornstarch and water.
Pour in the mixture and cook till the sauce becomes dense.
Serve topped with some more onions and pepper flakes if you wish.

NUTRITION INFORMATION
Calories: 145
Total fat: 5 g
Carbohydrate: 1.3 g
Protein: 8 g

Chicken with Capsicum Stew with Red chilies

Prep Time: 5 minutes
Cook Time: 10 minutes
Serve: 4

Ingredients:

2 Tablespoons olive oil
4 Chicken breasts, cut into small pieces
2 Finely chopped onion
1 Cup of water or chicken stock
1 Tablespoon soy sauce
4 Red dry chilies
Coriander
1 Green capsicum, diced, seeds removed
Salt to taste
1 Minced garlic clove

Directions:

Discard the skin of the chicken and cut into small pieces.
In an electric pressure cooker, add the oil, the onion following by garlic.
Add in the chicken, soy sauce and cover with lid.
Cook for only 5 minutes on medium heat.
Pour in the chicken stock or water and add the capsicum, red chilies, salt and stir well.
Cover again and cook for about 5 more minutes on medium heat.
Release the pressure naturally and serve hot over rice.

NUTRITION INFORMATION
Calories: 144
Total fat: 7.2 g
Carbohydrate: 5.2 g
Protein: 12 g

Vegetarian Recipes

Tomato Egg Almond milk/coconut milky quiche in Pressure Cooker

Prep Time: 5 minutes
Cook Time: 30 minutes.
Serve: 6

Ingredients:

12 Eggs, large
½ Teaspoon salt
½ Cup almond milk/coconut milk
3 Cups chopped baby spinach
¼ Teaspoon black pepper
3 Sliced onions
1 Cup diced tomato
¼ Cup shredded parmesan cheese
4 Tomatoes for topping

Directions:

Add 1 ½ cup of water in the pot after putting trivet in the bottom.

Whisk almond milk/coconut milk, egg, pepper and salt in a large bowl.

In another bowl, mix spinach, onions and tomato.

Pour the egg mixture on the veggies and stir well.

Place sliced tomatoes on top along with parmesan cheese.

Place the dish with a sling on the trivet, in the electric pressure cooker pot.

Lock lid and cook for 20 minutes on high pressure.

After beep, wait 10 minutes and have a quick pressure release.

Open the lid carefully, bring out the dish, broil till brown and then serve.

NUTRITION INFORMATION

Calories: 345

Total fat: 10.6 g

Carbohydrate: 16.4 g

Protein: 18.1 g

Easy homemade pumpkin puree in the Pressure Cooker

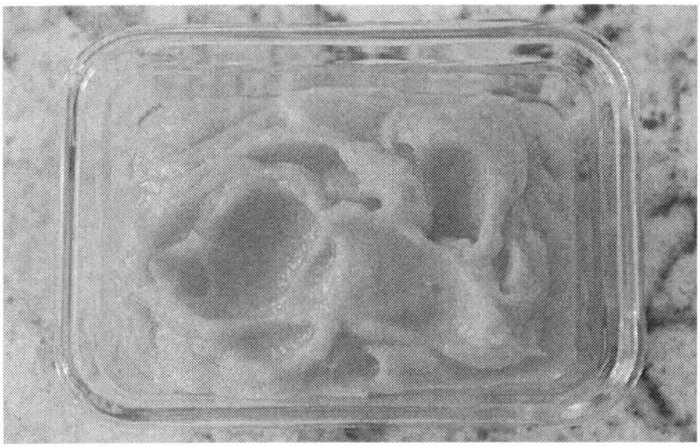

Prep Time: 2 minutes
Cook time: 20 minutes
Serve: 2-3 cups

Ingredients:

3 ½ cup to 4 pound pumpkin pie
1 cup water

Directions:

Make the pumpkin free from its stem.
Add 1 cup water and place the rack inside the electric pressure cooker.
Put the pumpkin on the rack.
Close the lid and cook for 13 minutes on high pressure.
Have a natural release.
Put out the pumpkin carefully and place it on a cutting board.
After cooling, cut it and get rid of the seeds and goop and peel the skin.

Blend it in a food processor and add water if necessary. Store it in the freezer till ready to use.

NUTRITION INFORMATION

Calories: 125

Total fat: 1.6 g

Carbohydrate: 6 g

Protein: 1.2 g

Quick Pressure Cooker Pumpkin Chili

Prep Time: 15 minutes
Cook Time: 1 hour
Serve: 6-8

Ingredients:

Pumpkin puree:
2 Tablespoons vegetable oil
1 Medium diced onion
4 Minced garlic cloves
1 Peeled, seeded and cut into 1 inch cubes pie pumpkin
¼ Cup chili powder
1 Teaspoon kosher salt
1 Teaspoon dried oregano
1 Tablespoon cumin
½ Cup of water
¾ Teaspoon baking soda
Chili:
1 Tablespoon minced chipotle
2 Cans diced tomatoes
8 Cups black beans, cooked

Salt and pepper to taste
2 Teaspoon brown sugar

Directions:

Heat the oil in the electric pressure cooker pot till shimmering.
Stir in garlic, pumpkin and onion and coat with almond butter.
Sprinkle with chili powder, oregano, salt and baking soda.
Stir again to coat the pumpkin well.
Add water, lock the lid, lower the heat and cook on high pressure for 20 minutes.
Have a quick release and remove the lid.
Stir in the black beans with liquid, chipotles en adobo, brown sugar and diced tomatoes and chilies.
Lock the lid and cook for 5 minutes on high pressure.
Have a quick release and remove the lid.
Serve after tasting chili and adding salt and pepper as your taste.

NUTRITION INFORMATION
Calories: 242
Total fat: 7.5 g
Carbohydrate: 18.5 g
Protein: 12 g

Quick Potato and Egg Salad with Herby Dressing

Prep Time: 10 minutes
Cook Time: 4 Minutes
Serve: 6

Ingredients:

2-2.5 Pounds peeled and cubed potatoes
4-5 Eggs
1-1.5 Cup water
For Dressing:
2 Tablespoon freshly chopped parsley
3 or 4 cup mayonnaise
1 Stalk of freshly chopped celery
2 Tablespoons of chopped dill pickles
1 Tablespoon of yellow mustard
¼ Cup of chopped scallion
1 Tablespoon of season salt
1 Tablespoon of sea salt

For garnishing:
1 Tablespoon of paprika

Directions:

Put raw potatoes in water and soak for 30 minutes.
Now drain them and with egg, put them all in steamer basket.
With water underneath, place it inside the electric pressure cooker.
Lock the lid and check the valve.
Cook on high pressure for 4 minutes.
Do a quick release with the beep sound.
Put the eggs in cold ice and potatoes in a large bowl.
Mix all the dressing ingredients and pour over potatoes.
Peel and chop the eggs, then add to potatoes.
Cover it and place it in fridge till ready to serve.

NUTRITION INFORMATION
Calories: 282
Total fat: 14.6 g
Carbohydrate: 15 g
Protein: 11.3 g

Pressure Cooker Roast Potatoes

Prep time: 5 minutes
Cook time: 15 minutes
Serve: 4

Ingredients:

1 Rosemary sprig
3 Garlic of cloves
Salt and pepper to taste
500 g baby potatoes
3 Tablespoon of olive oil
½ Cup vegetarian stock

Directions:

Add vegetable oil in the pre heated electric pressure cooker.
Add potatoes, rosemary and garlic to the heated oil.
For 8-10 minutes, roll the potatoes around so that the outside gets brown.
With a knife, make a hole in the middle of the potatoes.

Pour in the stock.
Close the lid and cook for 7 minutes on high pressure.
Release pressure on normal method; wait for 10 minutes to come the pressure down.
Remove all the outer skin of the garlic cloves.
To taste, sprinkle everything with salt and then serve.

NUTRITION INFORMATION
Calories: 185
Total fat: 0.6 g
Carbohydrate: 18 g
Protein: 1.6 g

Pressure Cooker Creamy Potatoes Soup

Prep time: 5 minutes
Cook time: 23 minutes
Serve: 10

Ingredients:

4 big potatoes, peeled and cut into cubes
4 small chopped onions
1½ cups of water
2 Teaspoon salt
¼ Teaspoon of pepper
4 Cups of almond milk/coconut milk
1 Tablespoon chopped parsley
3 Cups of grated cheddar cheese

Direction:

In electric pressure cooker, put water, potatoes, salt and onions.

Close the lid and on high heat, bring to full pressure.
After a while reduce heat and cook for 3 minutes.
Remove cooker off the heat and let it cool naturally till no pressure left inside.
In a blender, mix the mixtures smoothly.
Put the soup cooker again.
Add pepper and almond milk/coconut milk.
Put cooker on medium heat. Stir constantly and bring to boil.
Add cheese and keep stirring till it melts.
Garnish with parsley and serve instantly.

NUTRITION INFORMATION
Calories: 188
Total fat: 8 g
Carbohydrate: 16 g
Protein: 6.1 g

Easy Pressure Cooker Turmeric Cauliflower

Prep Time: 1 minute
Cook Time: 6 minute
Serve: 4

Ingredients:

1 green leaves removed whole cauliflower
½ Teaspoon of Turmeric
1.5 Cups of water
¼ Teaspoon of salt
½ Teaspoon of freshly ground pepper
3 chopped chives
1 tablespoon of almond butter

Directions:

Put water in electric pressure cooker pot.
Place the cauliflower in steamer basket.
Place the basket in the pot.
Close pressure valve after locking the lid.
For 6 minutes cook on the steam setting.
After beep sounds, let it have a natural pressure release for 2 minutes.
Release remaining pressure with a kitchen towel.
Mix the cauliflower in a food processor.
Add pepper, salt, almond butter and turmeric and bled till desired consistency.
With fresh chives, garnish.

NUTRITION INFORMATION
Calories: 129
Total fat: 2.6 g
Carbohydrate: 8.2 g
Protein: 1.1 g

Simple Pressure Cooker Beets

Prep Time: 10 minutes
Cook Time: 20 minutes
Serve: 6

Ingredients:

6 Beets of 1 ½ pounds
¼ Cup of crumbled blue cheese
½ Teaspoon fresh ground black pepper
½ Teaspoon of kosher salt

Directions:

Trim the beets and rinse to remove dirt. Be careful not to cut it, so that the beet juice doesn't leak.
In the electric pressure cooker, pour 1 cup of water into the pot and put the beets on a rack.
Lock the lid and cook for 24 minutes on high pressure.
Have a quick release.
Remove the lid and transfer the beets on a cutting board carefully.

Let it cool, then using a paper towel, peel the skins and pull off the roots.

Trim the stems and cut the beets into squares.

Put the beets in a bowl and sprinkle pepper and salt.

Top with crumbled blue cheese and serve.

NUTRITION INFORMATION

Calories: 135

Total fat: 5.6 g

Carbohydrate: 8 g

Protein: 4.3 g

Fancy Eggplant in the Pressure Cooker

Prep Time: 5 minutes
Cook Time: 10 minutes
Serve: 6

Ingredients:

1 Eggplant, cubed
2 Minced garlic cloves
1 Large seeded and diced red bell pepper
1 Large seeded and diced green bell pepper
1 Teaspoon dried oregano
1/2 Cup water
Pinch sugar
1 Teaspoon salt
1 Cup chopped onion
¼ Teaspoon parsley sprig
14 Oz diced tomatoes

Directions:

In the electric pressure cooker, sauté onions, peppers and garlic in hot oil till onions are soft.

Add eggplant and coat it with oil.

Then add thyme, sugar, water and salt.

Gently place the tomatoes on top.

Lock the lid and cook for 3 minutes on high pressure.

Use quick release after beep.

Stir remaining olive oil and parsley and then serve.

NUTRITION INFORMATION

Calories: 145

Total fat: 2.6 g

Carbohydrate: 11 g

Protein: 5.1 g

Pressure Cooker Eggplant Marinara

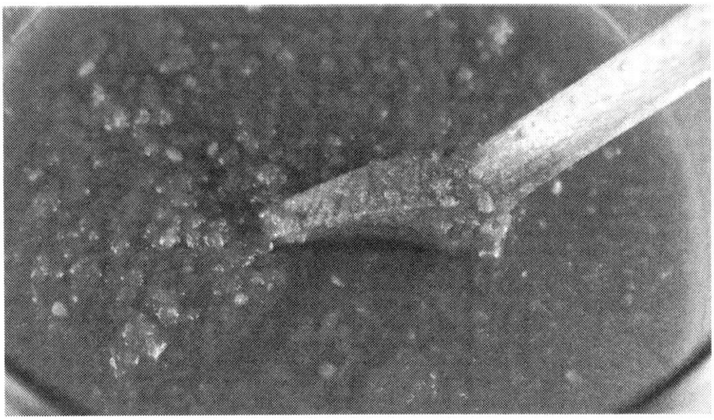

Prep Time: 10 minutes
Cook time: 8 minutes
Serve: 2

Ingredients:

1 Peeled eggplants
3 Minced of garlic cloves
1 Tablespoon of garlic powder
1 Tablespoon of olive oil
1 Cup of marinara sauce
Water as needed
Salt and pepper to taste

Directions:

Add all the ingredients to electric pressure cooker after sautéing garlic in olive oil.
Add water according to pressure cooker instructions.
Bring up to pressure after stirring and closing.

Then cook for 6-8 minutes.
Have a natural release.
Serve.

NUTRITION INFORMATION
Calories: 124
Total fat: 1.0 g
Carbohydrate: 5.2 g
Protein: 1.4 g

Casserole and Stew Recipes

Pressure Cooker Beef Brown Rice Casserole

Prep Time: 15 min
Cook Time: 15 min
Serve: 6-8

Ingredients:

1 tbsp olive oil
1 Red diced onion
1 lb ground beef
½ Tsp salt
1 tsp Chili powder
2 ½ Cups water
½ Cup brown rice
1 ½ Cups salsa
1 Can green chilies
1 Can drained black beans
1 Cup shredded cheese

Directions:

In the electric pressure cooker pot, heat the oil on high pressure and add meat when the oil is sizzling.
For 3 minutes brown the meat and then add chili powder, onion and salt. Keep cooking till the meat is barely brown.
Add salsa, water and rice. Close the lid.
Cook for 15 minutes on high pressure.
Have a quick release.
Add green chilies, corn and beans and cook on high pressure for another 5 minutes.
Drizzle with cheese. Serve hot.

NUTRITION INFORMATION

Calories: 185
Total fat: 8 g
Carbohydrate: 19 g
Protein: 8 g

Pressure Cooker Southwest pinto bean chard

Prep Time: 5 min
Cook Time: 15 min
Serve Time: 6

Ingredients:

1 Cup chopped onions
2 Tablespoons olive oil
1 Clove of minced garlic
4 Cups of vegetable broth
1 ½ Cups short grain Rice
1 ¾ Cups rinsed and drained beans
1 Small stem removed, leaved cleaned chard
¼ Teaspoon of red pepper flakes
½ Teaspoon of sea salt

Directions:

Heat the oil in electric pressure cooker pot.
Till the onions are brown, sauté them for 5 minutes.
Add rice and keep stirring to coat the grains.
Add 3 ½ cups vegetable broth.
Lock the lid and cook for 4 minutes on high pressure. Release the pressure instantly.
Start the heat again and add green chilies, beans, chard ribbons and ½ cup left broth.
Keep stirring till the beans are heated through and the chard has wilted.
Taste for salt and add red pepper flakes, then serve.

NUTRITION INFORMATION
Calories: 208
Total fat: 4.2 g
Carbohydrate: 26 g
Protein: 5 g

Pressure Cooker Pot Roast and Potatoes

Prep Time: 1 hour
Cook Time: 3 hour
Serve: 6

Ingredients:

Salt and pepper
1 Boneless trimmed beef chunk
1 tablespoon of vegetable oil
2 tablespoon tomato paste
1 finely chopped onion
½ Ounce of dried, rinsed and minced mushrooms
2 pounds small potatoes
2 cups of beef broth

Directions:

Season with pepper and salt, after patting beef dry with paper towels.
Add oil to the electric pressure cooker pot and select browning.
Brown for 8-10 minutes, the remove the platter.
Add onions and stir for 5 minutes. Stir mushroom and tomato paste and keep doing it till 3 minutes.
While the broth is simmering, scrape up the bottom of the pot.
Put the browned pot roast with the juice and put the potatoes on top of them.
Close the lid and cook for 90 minutes on high pressure for 15 minutes. Have a quick pressure release after the time.
Remove the lid and transfer the beef with the potatoes to serve the dish.
With aluminum foil, tent, beef loosely and let it rest for 15 minutes before carving.
Skim the juices and return it to the pressure cooking pot.
Select sauté and make gravy.

NUTRITION INFORMATION
Calories: 180
Total fat: 15.8 g
Carbohydrate: 18 g
Protein: 9.2 g

Pressure Cooker Black Beans with chorizo

Prep Time: 5 min
Cook Time: 1 hour
Serve: 6-8

Ingredients:

6 ounces Chorizo
1 tablespoon vegetable oil
1 split in half whole onion
1 pound dried black beans
6 garlic cloves
1 split in half orange
2 quarts chicken stock
2 bay leaves
Chopped fresh cilantro
2 teaspoon kosher salt

Directions:

Heat oil in the electric pressure cooker pot till shimmering.
Add chorizo and cook by stirring till it gets crisp for 2 minutes.
Add onions, orange, garlic cloves, bay leaves, beans and chicken stock and salt.
Cover and cook for 40 minutes on high pressure.
Allow pressure to have a natural release.
Remove lid and get rid of orange, onion and bay leaves.
Season with salt and pepper, then sprinkle cilantro.

NUTRITION INFORMATION
Calories: 220
Total fat: 6.2 g
Carbohydrate: 26 g
Protein: 7 g

Pressure Cooker Chicken and black bean stew

Prep time: 15 minutes
Cook Time: 1 hour
Serve: 4-6

Ingredients:

8 ounces smoked sausages
1 tablespoon vegetable oil
1 medium diced onion
2 can dice green chilies
2 teaspoon ground cumin
8 ounces dried black beans
4 chicken legs
12 stems leave roughly chopped cilantro
Kosher salt and ground pepper
1 quart chicken stock
Lime wedges to serve

Sour cream to serve

Directions:

Over medium high heat, heat oil in electric pressure cooking pot till shimmering.
Add sausages and cook till crisp for 2 minutes.
Add onions and cool till softened for 3 minutes.
Add cumin and cook till fragrant for 30 seconds.
Add cilantro, black beans, chilies, broth and chicken then season with pepper and salt; stir to combine.
Close the lid and cook for 40 minutes on high pressure.
Transfer chicken pieces to a bowl.
Get rid of cilantro.
Continue cooking after returning the bean on high heat, keep stirring till thickness for 5 minutes. Shred chicken from bones and also discard skin.
Add chicken in the bean season salt and pepper to taste and keep stirring. Add cilantro.
Serve with sour cream and lime wedges and remaining cilantro.

NUTRITION INFORMATION
Calories: 255
Total fat: 11.2 g
Carbohydrate: 23 g
Protein: 11 g

Soup recipes

Pressure Cooker Chicken Noodles

Prep Time: 5 min
Cook Time: 40
Serve: 2-4

Ingredients:

1 Small roughly diced onion
2 Boneless of chicken breasts
4 Cloves of roughly minced garlic
1 Bay of leaf
6chopped white button mushrooms
1 chopped of medium carrot
5-6 cups of chicken stock
1 chopped of celery stalk
1 Tablespoon of olive oil
Kosher salt
8 Ounce egg noodles

Ground black pepper
1 Tablespoon freshly squished lemon juice
¼ Cup finely chopped Italian parsley

Directions:

Prepare the electric pressure cooker with the sauté button. Add 1 tablespoon olive oil and sauté the mushrooms with kosher salt and ground black pepper.. When the mushrooms start to leave their moisture, add onions and garlic, then cook till onions start to smell. Then put carrot, celery and bay leaf. Season them with salt and pepper.
Pour 1/3 cup of chicken stock then stir very well to mix them all very well. Then add the remaining 2/3 cup of broth.
Now partially submerge the breasts of chicken and close the lid.
Cook for 7 minutes on high pressure and then has a natural release.
Open the lid and get rid of the bay leaf and shred the chicken with a fork.
Pour 4-5 cups chicken stock and press the sauté button to have various sauté functions and adjust to your taste.
Add egg noodles and cook for more 4-8 minutes. Then add salt, pepper and lemon juice to brighten.
Turn the heat off and add shredded chicken into the electric pressure cooker.
Serve instantly after garnishing with Italian parsley.

NUTRITION INFORMATION

Calories: 220

Total fat: 4.5 g

Carbohydrate: 24 g

Protein: 11 g

Pressure Cooker Spicy Chicken Soup

Prep time: 10 min
Cook time: 40 min
Serve: 1-2

Ingredients:

1 Large diced of onion
2 Tablespoon of olive oil
3 Cloves, minced and pressed garlic
1 Jar mild chunky salsa
4boneless chicken breast
2 Cans of peeled and diced tomatoes
½ Teaspoon of salt
2 Cans of chicken broth
1 Teaspoon op ground black pepper
1 Teaspoon of garlic powder
1 Tablespoon of onion powder
2 Tablespoon of dried parsley
1 Tablespoon of chili powder
1 Bag of frozen corn
2 Cans of drained black beans

Directions:

Select sauté to the electric pressure cooker and add olive oil. When oil gets hot, add onion and cook for 5 minutes till tender. Add garlic and cook for another minute.

Except corn and beans, add all the ingredients and then lock the lid. Cook for 8 minutes on high pressure.

When the beep makes sound, turn it off and wait for 10 minutes. Have a quick release.

Dice the chicken after removing it from soup, then return it and stir with corn and beans.

Select shimmer, bring to a boil till the corn and beans are heated.

Serve with sour crème, shredded cheese and tortilla soup being topped.

NUTRITION INFORMATION

Calories: 290

Total fat: 5 g

Carbohydrate: 21 g

Protein: 10 g

Butternut Squash Soup with Chicken and Orzo

Prep time: 10 min
Cook Time: 30 min
Serve: 2

Ingredients:

3 Tablespoon butter
1 ½ lbs Fresh baked butternut squash
½ Cup of diced green onions
½ Cup of dices carrots
½ Cup of diced celery
1 minced garlic clove
1 14.5 oz. can diced tomato with juice
2 14.5 oz. cans chicken broth
½ Teaspoon of Italian seasoning
1/8 Teaspoon of dried red pepper flakes
1/8 Teaspoon of freshly grated nutmeg
¼ Teaspoons of freshly ground black pepper
1 cup cooked orzo
Green onion sliced very thin tops
1 cup of cooked and dried chicken
1 cup of half and half

Directions:

Melt butter in the electric pressure cooker pot. Saute carrots, onions and celery. Stir briefly after adding garlic then add tomatoes and squash with chicken stock. Also add Italian seasoning, pepper, red pepper flakes and nutmeg.

Close the lid and cook on high pressure for 10 minutes. When beep sounds, switch it off and have a pressure release after 10 minutes.

After the valve drops, carefully remove the lid by tilting so that the steam disappear.

Pure till smooth mixture and then select shimmer and add orzo, chicken and half and half till chicken is heated.

Serve with thinly sliced green tops used for garnishing.

NUTRITION INFORMATION

Calories: 295

Total fat: 8 g

Carbohydrate: 14 g

Protein: 12 g

Split Pea Soup With Chicken Sausage

Prep Time: 10 min
Cook Time: 30 min
Serve: 6-8

Ingredients:

2 Tablespoon of butter
1 lb ground chicken sausage
1 Finely chopped onion
½ Cup diced carrots
½ Cup diced celery
2 Pressed and finely chopped garlic cloves
2 Cups of water
2 14-Ounce cans chicken stock
1 Package of rinsed and sorted split peas
½ Cup half and half
¼ Teaspoon of dried pepper flakes
Salt and fresh ground pepper

Directions:

In a electric pressure cooking pot, put sausages and select sauté. Put them in a plate after finished.

Melt butter in the pressure cooking pot then sauté carrots, onions and celery for 5 minutes till tender. Add garlic and cook for another minute and the add chicken stock, split peas, water and red pepper flakes.
Close the lid and cook on high pressure for 10 minutes. When the beep sounds, have a quick release after 10 minutes.
After the valve drops, carefully remove the lid and puree till smooth well.
Add half and half and sausages then select simmer till sausages heated. For taste, add pepper and salt.

NUTRITION INFORMATION

Calories: 240

Total fat: 6 g

Carbohydrate: 15 g

Protein: 11 g

Pressure Cooker Vegetable Beef and Rice Soup

Prep Time: 5 min
Cook Time: 15 min
Serve: 6

Ingredients:

1 Tablespoon of olive oil
1 lb lean ground beef
1 Large diced onion
1 Chopped rib celery
2 14 Ounce cans beef broth
3 Cloves finely chopped garlic
1 14- Ounce can crushed tomatoes
½ Cup of long grain white rice
1 12- Ounce bottle original v8 juice
1 15- Ounce can of drained and rinsed garbanzo beans
2 Peeled then sliced into thin cons carrots
1 Large peeled and diced into 1-inch pieces potato
½ Cup frozen and then thawed peas
Pepper and salt

Directions:

Preheat the electric pressure cooking pot using sauté function. Add ground beef and cook till browned. Transfer it to a plate on paper towels.
Add oil to the pressure cooking pot and then add celery and onion. Keep cooking for 5 minutes stirring often till onions are tender. Add garlic and cook another minute.
To the pot add carrots, beef broth, potatoes, tomatoes, browned ground beef, v8 juice, rice and garbanzo beans and stir to combine.
Lock the lid and cook for 4 minutes on high pressure. When the beep sounds, turn off and have a quick release.
Season with pepper and salt to taste after stirring in peas.

NUTRITION INFORMATION

Calories: 350

Total fat: 5.6 g

Carbohydrate: 40 g

Protein: 15 g

Creamy chicken wild Rice Soup

Prep Time: 5 min
Cook Time: 20 min
Serve: 6-8

Ingredients:

1 Cup of chopped onion
2 Tablespoons butter
1 Cup of diced carrots
2 14 Oz. cans chicken broth
1 Cup of diced celery
2 Large boneless skinless uncooked chicken breasts
1 Teaspoon of salt
6 Oz. package rice
½ Teaspoon of black pepper
1 Tablespoon of dried parsley

Dash red pepper flakes
2 Tablespoon of cornstarch
4 oz. cream cheese
2 Tablespoon of water
1 Cup half and half
1 Cup of milk

Directions:

Add butter to the electric pressure cooking pot and select sauté. Add onion, celery and carrot when the butter is melted and cook for 5 minutes till vegetables are tender.
Add chicken, parsley, salt, chicken broth, rice and pepper to the pot.
Lock the lid and cook for 5 minutes on high pressure. When the beep sounds have a quick release after waiting for 5 minutes.
Dissolve cornstarch in water about 2 Tablespoon in a small bowl. Select sauté and pour the mixture in the pot and keep stirring. Add cream cheese till melted. Finally add half milk and heat thoroughly but don't make it boiled.

NUTRITION INFORMATION
Calories: 289
Total fat: 12 g
Carbohydrate: 18.4 g
Protein: 14.5 g

Potato Bacon Chicken Butter Soup

Prep Time: 7 min
Cook Time: 20 min
Serve: 8

Ingredients:

6 Slices diced bacon
1 Tablespoon butter
1 Pound ground chicken sausages
1 Cup diced onion
3 Can of divided chicken broth
3 Cloves, minced garlic
½ Teaspoon of salt
1/8 Teaspoon of red pepper flakes
½ Teaspoon of black pepper
3 Large russet of cubed potatoes
1 Can of evaporated milk
3 Tablespoon corn of starch
2 cups fresh roughly chopped spinach

1 Cup Parmesan, shredded and divided cheese

Directions:

Add bacon to the electric pressure cooking pot and select sauté. Cook till crisp and transfer them to a plate with paper towel.

Put sausages to the pot and cook till brown. Transfer them on another plate with paper towel.

Now put the butter in the pot. When it melts, add onion, then cook for 5 minutes, stirring often till its tender. Add garlic and cook for another minute, then add red pepper flakes, salt, chicken broth and pepper.

Put steamer basket and potatoes and close the lid. Cook for 4 minutes on high pressure. When the beep sounds have a quick release, then remove the steamer basket and potatoes.

Add the remaining 2 cans of chicken broth to the pot.

In a little evaporated milk, dissolve cornstarch in another mixing bowl. Add this to the pressure cooking pot with the remaining milk. Bring to boil selecting simmer with occasional stirring. When it thickens, add spinach, potatoes, 3 or 4 cup of Parmesan cheese, half of the crispy bacon and browned sausages

Now serve with remaining bacon and Parmesan cheese.

NUTRITION INFORMATION

Calories: 320

Total fat: 8.5 g

Carbohydrate: 35 g

Protein: 18 g

Pressure Cooker Vegetable Beef Soup

Prep Time: 5 min
Cook Time: 10 min
Serve: 1-2

Ingredients:

1 Large diced onion
2 lbs lean ground beef
2 tsp minced garlic
3 Cups of beef broth
1 an with liquid stewed tomatoes
4 Sliced into round disks carrots
3-4 cut into bite-sized chunks medium-large potatoes
3 Stalks of sliced or diced celery
3 tbsp tomato paste
½ Tsp pepper
½ Tsp salt 1/2 tsp ground oregano
2 Tsp dried parsley flakes

Directions:

Turn the electric pressure cooker into sauté then add onion, ground beef and garlic. Saute till beef is cooked through then drain the oil.

With liquid, add can of stewed tomatoes. Break up tomatoes into small pieces, then stir in beef broth, tomato paste, diced vegetables and seasoning.

Close the lid and cook on high pressure for 4 minutes. When the valve drops, have a quick release.

Serve hot.

NUTRITION INFORMATION

Calories: 355

Total fat: 8.3 g

Carbohydrate: 32 g

Protein: 18 g

Pressure Cooker Buffalo Chicken Soup

Prep Time: 10 minutes
Cook time: 10 minutes
Serve: 2

Ingredients:

2 Boneless/skinless chicken breast
½ Cup of diced celery
3 Cups of chicken bone-broth
¼ Cup of diced onion
1 Tablespoon of ranch dressing mix
1 Clove of chopped garlic
2 Tablespoon of butter
1/3 Cup of hot sauce
1 Cup of heavy cream
2 cups cheddar, shredded cheese

Directions:

In the electric pressure cooker, mix all the ingredients except cheese and cream.
Close the lid and cook on high pressure for 10 minutes.
Remove the chicken carefully, shred it and then again return it to the soup.
Add cheese and heavy cream, then stir to combine.

NUTRITION INFORMATION

Calories: 315

Total fat: 10 g

Carbohydrate: 28.4 g

Protein: 16 g

Pot Chicken Tortilla Soup

Prep Time: 7 min
Cook Time: 15 min
Serve: 1-2

Ingredients:

2 Cans of drained but not rinsed beans
3 Chicken breasts
2 Cans of petite dried diced tomatoes
1 Medium diced onion
1 Diced bell pepper
4 Cups of chicken stock without salt
½ Bunch finely chopped cilantro
1 Tbsp chili powder
1 Tsp minced garlic
1 tbsp cumin
½ Tsp chipotle powder
Kosher salt
EVOO

Directions:

Turn the electric pressure cooker to sauté. Add EVOO 1 tbsp and cook bell peppers and onions for 5 minutes till the onions are brown. After starting to cook, season with kosher salt and a little grind of pepper. Add garlic and cook for another 2 minutes.

Add tomatoes, beans, cumin, chipotle, chili powder, ½ tsp freshly ground pepper and kosher salt. Mix well and then top with chicken breasts.

Now pour the 4 cups of chicken broth and add a handful chopped cilantro.

Close the lid and cook for 8 minutes on high pressure. Have a quick release, then shred the chicken. Return it after shredding and add salt and pepper as taste.

Serve after topping with tortilla chips, cheese and sour crème.

NUTRITION INFORMATION

Calories: 325

Total fat: 8 g

Carbohydrate: 28.5 g

Protein: 19.2 g

Indian Style Rice Lentil Carrot Soup

Prep Time: 10 min
Cook Time: 30 min
Serve: 4

Ingredients:

2 Cups of rice
1 Tbsp of cumin
½ Cups of chopped carrots
½ Bunch of finely chopped cilantro
6 Cups of water
1 Cup of lentils
Salt to taste
1 Medium diced onion
1 Tbsp chili powder
1 Tbsp butter
1 Tsp minced garlic

Directions:

In an electric pressure cooker, add the butter.
Fry the onion, and garlic for 2 minutes.
Add the lentils and rice and toss for 3 minutes.
Add all the spices and the stir well.
Add the vegetable and stir again.
Season using salt and pour in the water.
Stir well and cover with lid.
Cook for about 30 minutes with high pressure.
Serve with fresh cilantro on top.

NUTRITION INFORMATION

Calories: 311

Total fat: 4.6 g

Carbohydrate: 22.3 g

Protein: 11.5 g

Mixed Recipes

Spicy Chickpea potato Curry

Prep Time: 10 min
Cook Time: 1 hour
Serve: 6

Ingredients:

2 Cups of chickpeas
1 Tbsp cumin
½ Cup of chopped potatoes
1 Tbsp of paprika
½ Bunch of finely chopped coriander
1 Tbsp chili powder
4 Cups of water
1 Cup of sliced cucumber
Salt to taste
2 Diced onion
1 Tbsp oil

Directions:

In an electric pressure cooker heat the oil.
Add the chickpeas and toss for a minute.
Pour in the water and cover with the lid.
Cook with high pressure for 30 minutes.
Add all the remaining ingredients except cucumber and half the onion and stir well.
Cover again and cook for another 30 minutes with low pressure.
Release the pressure and serve hot with cucumber, coriander and onions on top.

NUTRITION INFORMATION

Calories: 285

Total fat: 1.6 g

Carbohydrate: 28 g

Protein: 2.5 g

Egg and Vegetable Fried Rice

Prep Time: 10 min
Cook Time: 30 min
Serve: 4

Ingredients:

2 Cups of rice
1 tbsp cumin
4 Eggs
½ Cups of chopped carrots
½ Cup of chopped cilantro
½ Cup of chopped celery
4 Cups of water
1 Tomato, to garnish
Salt to taste
½ Cup of chopped onion
2 Red chilies
2 Green chilies
1 Tbsp butter

Directions:

In an electric pressure cooker, add the butter and add the beaten eggs.
Make them scramble and transfer to a plate.
Add the rice, onion, and all the vegetables.
Add the chilies, spices and salt.
Stir for about 5 minutes and pour in the water.
Cover with lid and cook on high pressure for about 15 minutes.
Add the eggs and stir well. Add the herbs.
Toss for about 3 minutes.
Serve hot with tomatoes on top.

NUTRITION INFORMATION

Calories: 324

Total fat: 7.4 g

Carbohydrate: 27 g

Protein: 7.8 g

Raw Banana Curry

Prep Time: 10 min
Cook Time: 25 min
Serve: 4-6

Ingredients:

2 Cups of diced raw banana
1 Tbsp butter
2 Tbsp ginger garlic paste
4 Green chilies
1 Tbsp cumin
2 Tbsp curry powder
2 Tbsp chickpea flour
A handful of chopped herbs
4 Cups of water
1 Tbsp chili powder
Salt to taste
2 Diced onion
2 Tsp minced garlic

Directions:

In an electric pressure cooker melt the butter and fry the onion and garlic.
Add in the raw banana and toss for 2 minutes.
Add the rest of the ingredients one by one except the chickpea flour and herbs.
Cover and cook on medium pressure for about 20 minutes.
Add the herbs and chickpea flour and stir well for 5 minutes.
Serve hot with rice.

NUTRITION INFORMATION

Calories: 185

Total fat: 0.2 g

Carbohydrate: 12 g

Protein: 0.5 g

Spicy Egg Curry

Prep Time: 10 min
Cook Time: 30 min
Serve: 5

Ingredients:

5 Eggs
1 Tbsp ginger garlic paste
1 Tbsp onion paste
4 Green chilies or to taste
1 Tbsp cumin
1 Tbsp vegetable oil
Salt to taste
½ Cup of diced onion
1 Tbsp paprika

Directions:

In an electric pressure cooker hard boil the eggs with water for about 10 minutes with high pressure.
Drain well and let it cool down. Carefully discard the egg shells and set aside for now.
The same pressure cooker heat the vegetable oil over medium heat.
Fry the onion for a minute.
Add the onion paste, ginger garlic paste and all the spices.
Season using salt. Stir well and pour 1 cup of water.
Cover and cook on medium pressure for 5 minutes.
Add the hard boiled eggs and cover again.
Cook for another 8 minutes with low pressure.
Serve hot with rice.

NUTRITION INFORMATION

Calories: 186

Total fat: 2.5 g

Carbohydrate: 4.3 g

Protein: 7.5 g

Creamy Coconut Egg Gravy

Prep Time: 10 min
Cook Time: 30 min
Serve: 4

Ingredients:

4 Eggs
2 Cups of coconut milk
1 Tbsp ginger garlic paste
1 Tbsp vegetable oil
1 Tbsp onion paste
4 Green chilies or to taste
1 Tsp lemon juice
1 Tbsp grated coconut, (optional)
Salt to taste
½ Cup of diced onion

Directions:

In an electric pressure cooker, add the eggs carefully.
Pour enough water that covers all the eggs.
Cover with the lid and cook with medium pressure for about 8 minutes.
Release the pressure and drain the eggs. Pour cold water on top.
Discard the egg shells and transfer them to a plate.
In the same cooker heat the oil and add all the pastes.
Add the spices, green chilies and salt.
Pour the coconut milk and stir well.
Cover and cook for only 6 minutes.
Add the boiled eggs and cover again.
Cook on high pressure for about 12 minutes.
Check the thickness of the gravy, if you want it to be thicker, cook for another 4 minutes.
Serve hot.

NUTRITION INFORMATION

Calories: 289

Total fat: 5.8 g

Carbohydrate: 6 g

Protein: 11.5 g

Lobster Tail

Prep time: 1 min
Cook Time: 3 min
Serve: 2-4

Ingredients:

1 c. Water
Butter
1-2 lbs, lobster tails
Celtic Sea salt

Directions:

In the electric pressure cooking pot, place steamer basket and trivet with water.
Cut the lobster tail from to tail with a knife
In a steamer basket, place the lobster tail putting the shell side down.
Close the lid, and cook on high heat but low pressure.
Then reduce heat to medium low.
Let it steam for 3 minutes then have a quick release

Put the lobsters on a plate. Serve with melted butter and salt.

NUTRITION INFORMATION
Calories: 210
Total fat: 4 g
Carbohydrate: 8 g
Protein: 11 g

Pressure Cooker Risotto with shrimp Herbs

Prep Time: 5 min
Cook Time: 20 min
Serve: 1-2

Ingredients:

1 Small finely chopped yellow onion
4 Tablespoons unsalted undivided butter
2 Cloves of minced garlic
2 Tablespoons of vinegar
1 ½ Cups of Arborio Rice
4 ½ Cups of low-sodium undivided chicken broth
1 Pound shrimp
Coarse salt and freshly ground pepper
¼ Cup of chopped fresh herbs
¾ Cup of cheese

Directions:

Peel the shrimps and define them.
In the electric pressure cooker pot, on medium heat, melt 2 Tablespoons butter.
Stir after adding garlic and onion for 4 minutes.
Then add rice and cook for another minute.
Add wine and cook till evaporated, for like 30 seconds and then add pepper, broth and salt.
Close the lid and cook on medium-high pressure for 9 minutes till the rice is tender. When the beep sounds, have a quick release.
Open the lid, stir the remaining 1 ½ cup of broth and shrimp and cook till shrimp is brown.
Stir in remaining 2 Tablespoons of butter and cheese for 3-5 minutes.
Serve with herbs and more cheese.

NUTRITION INFORMATION

Calories: 390

Total fat: 8 g

Carbohydrate: 22 g

Protein: 16 g

Tasty Pressure Cooker shrimp Risotto

Prep Time: 20 minutes
Cooking Time: 15 minutes
Servings: 6-8

Ingredients:

2 Tablespoons of frozen shrimp
2 Cups of uncooked rice
1 Teaspoon of turmeric
2 Cups of chicken stock
1 Teaspoon of garlic powder
6 Ounces of creamy chicken soup
1 Large finely chopped onion
Salt and pepper to taste
1 Teaspoon of chili powder

Directions:

In an electric pressure cooker dump in the rice, chicken soup, chicken stock, onion, chili powder, turmeric and shrimp.
Season with salt and pepper.
Stir well and cover with the lid.

Set the timer to 12 minutes with medium heat.
Wait for the pressure cooker to release the pressure naturally.
Let it sit in the cooker 15minutes before serving.

NUTRITION INFORMATION

Calories: 189
Total fat: 8.6 g
Carbohydrate: 13.2 g
Protein: 10.1 g

Easy Pressure Cooker Lentil Rice

Prep Time: 10 minutes
Cooking Time: 10 minutes
Servings: 4

Ingredients:

1 cup lentils
Salt to taste
2 Green chilies
2 Tablespoon of turmeric
3 Red chilies
Fresh herbs
4 Tablespoon of olive oil
1 ½ Cups of rice
4 onions, diced
½ Teaspoon of cumin

Directions:

Add the olive oil in an electric pressure cooker.
Add the lentils and the rice with turmeric and diced onion.
Toss for 5 minutes and add the rest of the ingredients.

Stir well and add the cooker's lid.
Set the timer to 10 minutes with the pressure to high.
Release the pressure naturally.
Keep it in the cooker for 10 minutes before serving.

NUTRITION INFORMATION

Calories: 192
Total fat: 2.1 g
Carbohydrate: 12.3 g
Protein: 5.6 g

Shrimp Sacmpi Paella

Prep Time: 5 min
Cook Time: 10 min
Serve: 4

Ingredients:

1 Cup of jasmine rice
1 Pound frozen shrimp
¼ Cup of butter
1 Teaspoon of sea salt
¼ Cup chopped fresh parsley
1 Pinch crushed red pepper
¼ Teaspoon black pepper
1 Medium juiced lemon
1 ½ Cups chicken broth
1 Pinch saffron
4 Cloves of minced garlic

Directions:

In the electric pressure cooker, combine all the ingredients, keeping the shrimp on top.
Close the lid and cook on high pressure for 5 minutes.
Have a quick depressurize.
Carefully remove the shrimps from the rice and peel, then return to the rice and serve.
Serve with butter, fresh parsley, squeeze of lemon juice and grated cheese.

NUTRITION INFORMATION

Calories: 190

Total fat: 8 g

Carbohydrate: 4.4 g

Protein: 15 g

Pressure Cooker Spicy Chicken

Prep Time: 20 minutes
Cooking Time: 20 minutes
Servings: 6

Ingredients:

1 Whole chicken
4 Red dice onions
1 Tablespoon of turmeric
½ Teaspoon of cumin
½ Teaspoon of coriander
2 tablespoon ginger garlic paste
1 cup water
2 green chilies
Salt to taste
1 teaspoon chili powder
2 tablespoon olive oil
Fried onions to garnish

Directions:

Discard the skin of the chicken.
Cut the chicken into bite size pieces.
In an electric pressure cooker, add the olive oil.
Add the diced onion with ginger garlic paste, cumin, turmeric, cumin, coriander and chili powder.
Stir for a minute and add the water.
Mix well and cover with lid.
Set the timer to 5 minutes with medium pressure.
Release the pressure and add the chicken.
Season using salt and pepper.
Add the chilies and stir well.
Cover again and set the timer to 12 minutes with medium pressure.
Let the pressure release manually.
Serve the dish hot with rice on the side.

NUTRITION INFORMATION

Calories: 184
Total fat: 8.5 g
Carbohydrate: 3.2 g
Protein: 9.2

Pressure Cooker Spicy shrimp

Prep Time: 10 min
Cook Time: 15 min
Serve: 2-4

Ingredients:

½ Lemon juice
500g Fresh shrimp
500g Whole fresh tomatoes
1 Minced Onion
2 Garlic, minced cloves
4 Finely chopped fresh thyme sprigs
4 Tablespoons extra virgin olive oil
1 Jalapeno, minced pepper
1 Bay leaf
Fresh parsley
Salt

Directions:

Peel the shrimp, clean the thoroughly, drain and put them on a plate after being sprayed with lemon juice.
Scald, drain, put under cold water and then peel and chop the tomatoes.
Prep the onion, garlic, hot pepper and thyme.
Heat oil in the electric pressure cooking pot and make sauté the minced mix and bay leaf for 3 minutes.
Add shrimp and diced tomatoes.
Close the lid and cook on high pressure for 7 minutes.
Turn the heat off and have a quick release.
Thicken sauce for 2 minutes with the pot uncovered on high heat.
Get rid of the bay leaf. Serve with parsley.

NUTRITION INFORMATION

Calories: 185

Total fat: 6 g

Carbohydrate: 2.4 g

Protein: 16 g

Dessert Recipes

Carrot Pudding

Prep Time: 10 min
Cook Time: 30 min
Serve: 4

Ingredients:

4 Tablespoons of cashew, chopped
1 1/2 cup of grated carrots
2 Tablespoons of butter
2 Tablespoons of almonds, chopped
4 Cups of coconut milk
Sugar in accordance with the taste

Directions:

In an electric pressure cooker, add the butter.
Add the carrots and toss for about 3 minutes.
Pour in the coconut milk and stir well.

Cover with lid and cook with low pressure for about 10 minutes.

Add in the sugar and stir well.

Cover and cook for another 5 minutes.

Add the nut and stir well.

Take off the heat and serve cold.

NUTRITION INFORMATION

Calories: 240

Total fat: 4.6 g

Carbohydrate: 9.5 g

Protein: 8.5 g

Quick Semolina Pudding

Prep Time: 10 min
Cook Time: 10 min
Serve: 4

Ingredients:

1/2 Cup of semolina
2 Tablespoons of walnuts, minced
3 Cups of coconut milk
2 Tablespoons of almonds, Minced
2 Tablespoons of butter
Honey to taste

Directions:

In an electric pressure cooker melt the butter.
Add the semolina and toss until toasted.
Pour in the coconut milk, and stir well.
Cover with lid and cook for about 5 minutes.

Add in the honey, walnuts and almond.
Stir again and cook for another 2 minutes.
Serve cold.

NUTRITION INFORMATION
Calories: 175
Total fat: 6.8 g
Carbohydrate: 4.4 g
Protein: 5.5 g

Lemon Egg Coconut Flan

Prep Time: 10 min
Cook Time: 20 min
Serve: 4

Ingredients:

3 Eggs
2 Cups of coconut milk
1 Tsp lemon zest
1/2 Cup of brown sugar
1 Cup of water

Directions:

In a bowl, whisk the eggs and make it fluffy.
Combine the coconut milk with the eggs.
Mix in the brown sugar and mix well. Make sure it has dissolved completely.

Add the lemon zest and mix again.
Pour into greased round cake pan.
Pour about 1 cup of water in an electric pressure cooker.
Add a trivet onto your electric cooker.
Add the cake pan carefully and cover.
Cook with high pressure for about 20 minutes.
Release the pressure and let it cool down before taking it out of the cake pan.

NUTRITION INFORMATION

Calories: 180

Total fat: 2.5 g

Carbohydrate: 5.4 g

Protein: 11 g

Pistachio Carrot Cakes

Prep Time: 10 min
Cook Time: 20 min
Serve: 4

Ingredients:

2 Cups of grated carrot
2 Tbsp pistachio paste
A handful of pistachio
1 Tbsp rose water
1 Cup of milk
1 Cup of heavy cream
Honey to taste

Directions:

In an electric pressure cooker, pour in the milk.
Add the grated carrot, pistachio paste and rose water.
Stir well and cover with lid.
Cook for about 10 minutes with high pressure.

Add in the heavy cream, and honey. Mix again and cover. Cook for another 5 minutes and add the pistachios and mix. Serve cold.

NUTRITION INFORMATION

Calories: 150

Total fat: 6 g

Carbohydrate: 6 g

Protein: 8.5 g

Almond Rice Jaggery Rice pudding

Prep Time: 10 min
Cook Time: 30 min
Serve: 6

Ingredients:

4 Cups of Soy milk
1 Cup of melted Jaggery
1/2 Teaspoon of cinnamon
½ Cup of chopped almonds
1 teaspoon of raisins
1 tablespoons almond butter
1 cup of rice
1 dash of salt

Directions:

In an electric pressure cooker, add the almond butter with the rice.
Toss for a minute and add the cinnamon, salt, jaggery, and soy milk.
Mix everything together and cover with the cooker's lid.
Cook on medium pressure for 15 minutes.
Add the raisins and almonds and toss for 2 more minutes.
Serve cold.

NUTRITION INFORMATION

Calories: 210

Total fat: 6 g

Carbohydrate: 20 g

Protein: 12 g

Raw papaya Sweet Treats

Prep Time: 10 min
Cook Time: 20 min
Serve: 4

Ingredients:

4 Cups of milk
½ Cup of raw honey
Pomegranate to garnish
1 Dash of salt
Nuts to garnish
1/2 Teaspoon of cinnamon
1 Cup of grated raw papaya
1 Tablespoon of butter

Directions:

In an electric pressure cooker melt the butter.
Fry the grated papaya for about 3 minutes.
Pour in the milk and add the cinnamon.

Cover with lid and cook on medium pressure for about 8 minutes.
Add in the honey, and cover again.
Cook for another 4 minutes.
Transfer to a bowl and let it cool down.
Use your hands to make flat balls.
Add the nuts, pomegranate and serve cold.

NUTRITION INFORMATION

Calories: 180

Total fat: 3.4 g

Carbohydrate: 15 g

Protein: 6 g

Thank you

for buying our book!

I hope Air Fryer Cookbook is helpful for you!

I am constantly looking for way to improve my content to give readers the best value so If you didn't like the book I would like to also hear from you! Please feel free to give your honest opinions as this could help me make improvements.

Finally, if you enjoyed this book, would you be kind enough to leave a review for this book on Amazon?

Thank you and good luck!

Printed in France by Amazon
Brétigny-sur-Orge, FR

10400020R10087